WHY WE CRY

THE SCIENCE OF TEARS

BY MATT LILLEY

Consultant:
Eric H. Chudler, Ph.D.
Research Associate Professor
Department of Bioengineering
University of Washington
Seattle, WA

COMPASS POINT BOOKS
a capstone imprint

Published by Capstone,
1710 Roe Crest Drive, North Mankato, Minnesota 56003
www.capstonepub.com

Editorial Credits
Gina Kammer, editor, Kellie M. Hultgren, editor; Brann Garvey,
designer; Tracy Cummins, media researcher; Tori Abraham,
production specialist

Photo Credits
iStockphoto: tuaindeed, 36; Newscom: Gie Knaeps/LFI/
Photoshot, 35; Science Source: BO VEISLAND, 17, Zephyr, 44;
Shutterstock: 32 pixels, 46-47, Andrea Raffin, 38, Anneka, 13,
anyamuse, 49, Blamb, 18, Borysevych.com, 34, cheapbooks,
Cover, 5, 21, Daisy Daisy, 51, Dan Rentea, 25, Designua, 43,
GagliardiPhotography, 30, George Rudy, 53, Mastering_
Microstock, 10, Monkey Business Images, 45, Rawpixel.com, 37,
56-57, Roman Bodnarchuk, 40, rusty426, 23, Sebastian Kaulitzki,
42, Veja, 26-27, Vishnevskiy Vasily, 9, wavebreakmedia, 33,
Zhukova Valentyna, 6-7

Library of Congress Cataloging-in-Publication Data
 Names: Lilley, Matt, author.
 Title: Why we cry : the science of tears / by Matt Lilley.
 Description: North Mankato, Minnesota : Compass Point
  Books, [2020] | Series: Decoding the mind
 Identifiers: LCCN 2019004145 | ISBN 9780756561758
  (hardcover) | ISBN 9780756562205 (paperback) | ISBN
  9780756561970 (ebook pdf)
 Subjects: LCSH: Crying—Juvenile literature. | Crying—
  Physiological Aspects—Juvenile literature. | Emotions—
  Juvenile literature.
 Classification: LCC BF575.C88 L55 2020 | DDC 152.4—dc23 LC
  record available at https://lccn.loc.gov/2019004145

Printed in the United States of America.
PA71

Table of Contents

CHAPTER 1

Introduction: Only Humans

WHETHER OR NOT we want to admit it, some things just make us cry. We may blame a speck of dust, chopping an onion, or even smoke getting into our eyes. Maybe it's something sad in a book, as in the Harry Potter series when a certain character dies trying to save Harry (no spoilers!). Or maybe it's that moment in *Moana* with her and her grandmother (if you've seen it, you know the one). Whatever it is, if something triggers the right emotions, the tears flow.

Crying isn't always about sadness. All sorts of strong emotions can bring tears to people's eyes.

WE CRY:

- Out of anger or frustration
- Because of a broken friendship or romantic breakup
- Because a person or a pet has died
- Because of sad memories
- When someone hurts our feelings
- From losing a big game
- Out of joy, perhaps from celebrating a new addition to the family or a graduation

What is crying all about, really? Well, to answer that, it might help to first look at who cries. The answer: EVERYONE! A few medical conditions can prevent crying, but if you don't have those conditions, you probably cry.

Most animals, on the other hand, don't cry, even though they can produce tears to protect their eyes. Many animals can do things *like* crying—dogs can whimper, and chimpanzees can pout. But so far, with just a few possible exceptions, only humans are known to produce tears caused by strong emotions.

That makes crying one of the few distinctively human traits (like blushing). That's a clue that crying, on a very basic level, has something to do with being human. Maybe by learning about crying we can learn more about what it means to be human. Let's keep that in mind as we explore the science of tears.

DO ELEPHANTS CRY?

People have claimed that some animals, such as dogs, horses, and whales, can cry. Elephants are one of the animals most often labeled as criers. Elephants are highly social. Female elephants stick together in a herd led by the oldest and largest female. They can communicate over long distances. When an elephant in a herd dies, the other elephants mourn the death. Their heads go down, their ears droop, and they mope.

In 2013 a baby elephant in a zoo was attacked by his mother. The calf had to be removed from her for protection. Reportedly, he cried for about five hours. Photographs seem to show tears streaming from his eyes.

So yes, it's possible that some animals may cry. But if it happens, it's extremely rare. The report of the crying baby elephant is what scientists call anecdotal evidence. That means evidence that is based on personal accounts that have not been scientifically tested. Anecdotal evidence might or might not be true, so scientists don't like to draw conclusions from it.

Humans have three types of tears: basal tears, reflex tears, and emotional tears. Basal tears provide moisture to the eyes. Reflex tears are created in response to an injury, such as when your eyes are poked or irritated by a chemical. Emotional tears are produced by joy, anger, or sadness.

CHAPTER 2

Crybabies and Beyond Babies

TO UNDERSTAND WHY humans cry, it helps to look at how crying starts. Do you remember the first time you cried? Of course not—you were a baby! All babies cry. When babies are born, parents listen hopefully for the sound of crying. For the parents, the cries usually say, "I'm here! I'm healthy!" The sound of a baby's wail might even make the parents cry out of joy.

When you were a baby, there were a lot of things you couldn't do. You couldn't talk. You couldn't walk. At first, you couldn't even lift your head! You needed a lot of help. One thing babies are really good at is asking for help. But since they can't talk, they cry. When they're hungry, they cry. When they're uncomfortable, they cry. When they're lonely, they cry. Crying is an important emotional signal for babies *and* for their parents, so they know when to help.

Humans aren't unique in needing help as babies. Young birds and mammals also need their parents. They usually call out in some way if they are separated. But humans are unique in *how much* and *for how long* they need their parents. For at least the first two years of life, humans depend more on their parents for survival than the young of any other primate species do. This need for support continues through adolescence. The need for love and companionship is built in from the start—and it lasts throughout adulthood.

Now imagine that someone is asking for your help. All. The. Time. Day and night. That's babies. They are exhausting. But no matter how tired the parents are, the baby needs them nearby, ever ready. In order to survive, babies have to be really good at getting help. A simple separation cry, like the ones birds and mammals use, isn't enough. Tears take it to the next level.

That next level, beyond calling for help, is creating connections. Babies are masters at doing that. Crying—along with other social behaviors such as smiling, clinging, and making eye contact—is a key to making connections. One study found that during an infant's first three months, 75 percent of the baby's cries began when the mother wasn't nearby. Separations are the most likely trigger for crying. Sometimes instead of a physical need, such as a dry diaper, the baby is saying, "I need *you*." That's how important the caregiver's presence is.

When you were an infant, you cried automatically. Crying was involuntary, like a heartbeat. After about three months, you learned to control your crying. Along with your other communications, crying became more intentional. Three months is about the age when babies develop other interactive abilities, like smiling. They crave human connection. They are already learning social skills.

Imagine this sequence: Baby is hungry. Baby cries. Mom picks up and feeds baby. Baby and mom make eye contact. Mom talks to baby in a gentle voice. Baby smiles and babbles with mom. It sounds simple, but a lot happened there.

First, when a stressed-out baby cries, the mom immediately reacts. Studies have shown that the sound of a baby crying raises a person's blood pressure and is similar to hearing a smoke alarm. Crying puts both baby and mom into similar emotional states. You could say they're stressing out together. Then mom springs into action.

Right away, the sound of crying boosts the mom's levels of the hormone oxytocin. Oxytocin is sometimes called the love hormone. It increases a mom's milk production, and it also reduces stress and promotes bonding. Mothers with more oxytocin in their blood form stronger bonds with their babies. So with the oxytocin flowing, the mom feeds the baby.

Once the baby is fed, baby and mother are calm and quiet together. The baby will often make eye contact with the mom. They will smile and "talk" to each other. To the mom, it feels as if the baby has taken all the love she has given and is giving it right back. For moms, these can be magical moments. They make all the backaches and sleepless nights seem worth it.

So, all that crying is stressful, but when it works right, it leads to a stronger bond. After mom and baby feel stress together, they share special moments. They form love. This not only leads to a stronger bond, but also teaches the baby how bonds are created. The baby learns how to interact and make loving connections.

This isn't the only way for babies to make strong social connections. Not all moms breastfeed. Many times, the mom isn't the main caregiver. As long as babies have caring adults looking after them, strong bonds can still form. But scientists think crying evolved by helping to create this strong connection between mother and child.

However, what if the connection process doesn't take place? A lot can happen to disrupt it. There might be a physical separation. Physical or mental health problems in the parents or the baby can prevent this process from playing out. If that happens, the normal cycle of crying and connection might not be completed. The baby might miss its chance to experience love and a human-to-human connection.

Studies show that babies who miss out on this process can struggle later in life. Growing up, such a child is more likely to have mental health problems such as depression.

Our early experiences—even ones we don't remember—can have big effects on us later. But nothing is set in stone. One of the great things about the brain is that it always can change. So while some people's early experiences may increase their chances of having problems such as depression, that doesn't mean they can't cope and heal.

After mom and baby feel stress together, they share special moments. They form love.

"The first step to connection is communication."

Sabrina Benaim, writer, poet, and creator of the viral video "Explaining My Depression to My Mother"

13

Beyond Babies

A 6-year-old probably won't cry every time his or her mom leaves the room. A grown-up won't cry after not eating for three hours (usually). The reasons we cry change as *we* change. Here are some of the most common reasons people cry at different ages:

BABY

- Experiencing separation anxiety
- Feeling hungry or tired
- Having physical discomfort or pain

TODDLER

- Experiencing separation anxiety
- Feeling more frustration (from wanting to do things without help, but struggling)
- Feeling jealousy or embarrassment

ELEMENTARY SCHOOL

- Having disagreements with peers
- Developing empathy (feeling what another person feels, such as sadness)

ADOLESCENCE

- Continuing to develop empathy
- Experiencing stress from a greater desire for independence
- Experiencing new stresses from romantic feelings and relationships

ADULTHOOD

- Continuing to develop empathy
- Feeling sentimental in response to acts of other people, such as heroism and self-sacrifice
- Reacting to joy
- Responding to feelings of awe or wonder

These are examples of when we cry and what we cry about, but there are exceptions. As we grow and change from babies into adults, our connections spread from our parents, to our friends, and eventually to our communities. As these relations change, our reasons for crying change. The one constant is that it's all about connections. Through it all, tears help us form and protect these important connections.

THE MICHAEL JORDAN OF MEMES

On September 11, 2009, Michael Jordan was inducted into the NBA Hall of Fame. During his acceptance speech, he shed some tears.

A few years later, a photograph of Jordan crying was used as a meme. Once that happened, it took off. Soon Jordan's crying face was showing up all over the internet. Now there's even an app called the "Crying Jordan Meme Generator." Anyone can easily riff on the meme. But what does the meme mean?

The name Michael Jordan signifies "the best." When Barack Obama awarded Jordan the Presidential Medal of Freedom, he described Jordan as "more than just a logo—more than just an internet meme. . . . Because Michael Jordan is the Michael Jordan of greatness. He is the definition of somebody so good at what they do that everybody recognizes it."

If we think men are supposed to be too tough to cry, then seeing Jordan cry can be surprising. Sometimes, the internet is a mean place. Many people online like to make fun of stuff, especially people. It's not surprising that Jordan's emotional moment would be used to make fun of him.

When Jordan's crying face is placed over a picture of someone else's face, it's often saying that the person failed, that he or she should cry. But the meme isn't always used in a mean way. Sometimes people use it to make fun of themselves. The meme can be a playful way to say, "We lost." It also says that everyone, even Michael Jordan, fails—and everyone cries. The meme is proof that if we ever cry, or get picked on by an online bully, then we're a little bit like Jordan himself, the greatest of all time.

CHAPTER 3

The Biology of Tears

IF YOU THINK ABOUT IT, tears might seem kind of weird. People get emotional and liquid comes out of their eyes? What's actually going on in the brain? To get into that, let's look at how tears are produced.

The chemical in onions that makes us cry is called *lachrymatory-factor synthase*. Onions evolved to produce the chemical, which helps to protect them from being eaten. Unfortunately for onions, a lot of people think they're tasty enough that they're worth risking a few tears.

The Hardware

Tears are made by the lacrimal system, which works like this:
- The main lacrimal gland makes most of our tears. It is at the top of the eye.
- The lacrimal gland sends the tears to the surfaces of the eyes.
- Tear ducts at the inside corners of the eyes drain tears away (eventually they go into the nose).
- The lacrimal system sometimes makes more tears than the ducts can carry away. When this happens, you cry, like an overflowing sink.

Since tears build up at the tear ducts, which are visible (they start at those little spots in each inside corner), a lot of people think the ducts actually make the tears, but they don't.

Lacrimal System

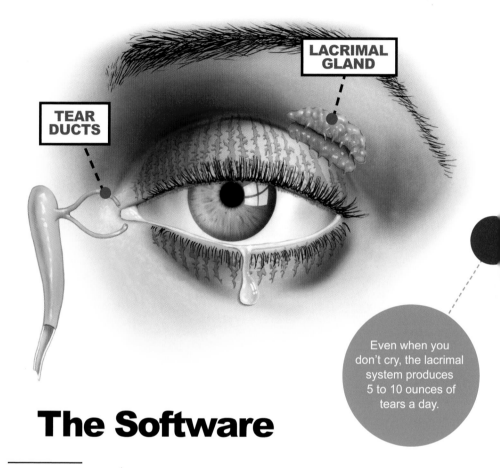

LACRIMAL
GLAND

TEAR
DUCTS

Even when you don't cry, the lacrimal system produces 5 to 10 ounces of tears a day.

The Software

Crying can happen in various ways. It might be a single tear in your right eye that you blink away. Or it could be heaving sobs and tears that flow and flow. Either way, emotional tears come when emotions are so strong that your brain tells the lacrimal system to start crying. The part of the brain that triggers crying is called the limbic system. The limbic system is the "emotional brain." It includes all the parts of your brain that process emotions.

So the lacrimal system is like a computer's hardware—the physical stuff that does something. The emotions in the limbic system are like the software—the computer program that tells the lacrimal system what to do.

The Limbic System

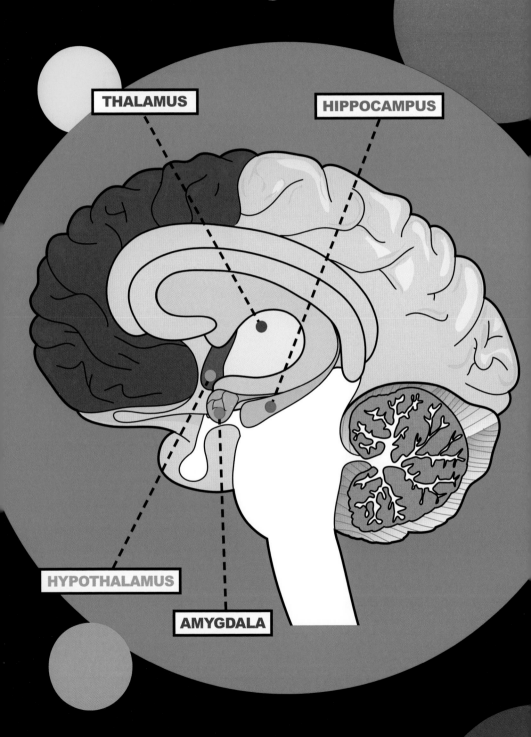

THALAMUS

HIPPOCAMPUS

HYPOTHALAMUS

AMYGDALA

The limbic system has many parts, but these are some of the main ones:

- **HIPPOCAMPUS:** This part of the brain is important for creating memories, especially spatial memories. This kind of memory helps us locate things and plan a route to somewhere. The hippocampus is essential to learning. It helps convert short-term memories into long-term memories. It has two halves, one on each side of the brain.

- **HYPOTHALAMUS:** The main job of the hypothalamus is to maintain homeostasis. Maintaining homeostasis just means staying balanced and healthy. For instance, if the body gets too hot, then the body tells the hypothalamus. The hypothalamus responds by sending the body signals to start sweating. The hypothalamus can also control things like appetite, thirst, and heart rate.

  One of the main ways the hypothalamus works is by creating and controlling certain hormones (such as oxytocin) that circulate in the body. The body system that controls hormones is called the endocrine system. The hypothalamus is part of the limbic system *and* the endocrine system—emotions and hormones, connected by the hypothalamus. The hypothalamus is like a command center, taking in information from the rest of the brain and then sending signals, directing your response.

- **AMYGDALA:** The amygdala is important for memory, but instead of spatial memory, it is more involved in "autobiographical" memory. Autobiographical memories are the memories of events in your life. Part of that is your emotional memory. Emotional memory tells us how something felt. Beyond just what happened to us, we can remember what it felt like. Were we scared? Happy? Sad? The amygdala is involved with creating memories with emotional codes such as anger, pleasure, sadness, and fear. The amygdala also handles social processing, especially involving faces. When we see a face, what emotions do we feel? If someone is looking at us, what is he or she thinking? Is the person a harmful enemy or a helpful friend? The amygdala helps us figure that out.

- **THALAMUS:** The thalamus is a relay station for all of your senses except smell. It takes in information from your senses and routes it to various parts of the brain, including the cerebral cortex (which controls voluntary movements).

What Happens in the Limbic System?

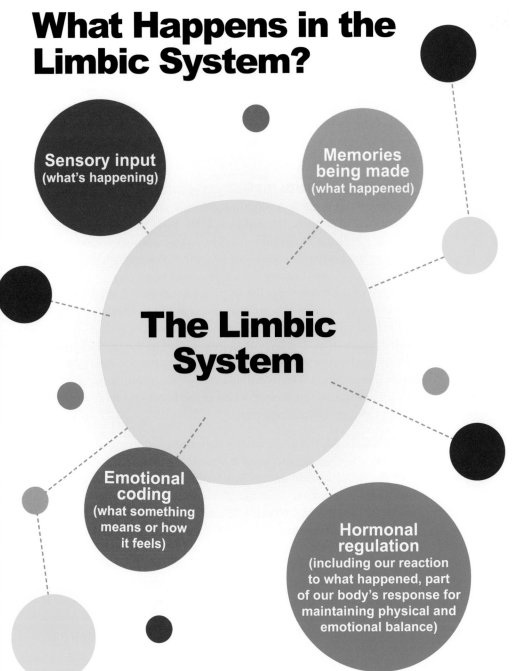

Sensory input
(what's happening)

Memories being made
(what happened)

The Limbic System

Emotional coding
(what something means or how it feels)

Hormonal regulation
(including our reaction to what happened, part of our body's response for maintaining physical and emotional balance)

When the limbic system is telling us that it all just feels like too much, it sends a message to the lacrimal gland: "We can't take it anymore! We need to cry!"

Brain scans show that physical pain activates some of the same parts of the brain that emotional pain does. This might be why we associate the two (and call them both pain), even though they are very different kinds of feelings. This also might be why both kinds of pain make us cry.

What Crying Does in the Brain

What does crying actually do? Is crying good for us? The short answer is that it's complicated.

Magazine articles sometimes say crying removes toxins and stress hormones from your blood. Some claim that crying releases endorphins (hormones that dull pain and make us feel happy). These statements haven't been proven, and the science is unclear.

Experts aren't sure about these claims, but they have other theories. One involves the hypothalamus. The hypothalamus is the command center of the brain. It listens to what's happening and prepares us for action. For instance, under extreme stress, it turns on the "fight-or-flight" response. Say you're walking in the woods and see a mountain lion. The hypothalamus sends signals that release adrenaline and other hormones into your blood, causing changes such as a rapid heartbeat. Suddenly you feel the urge to either fight or run away. Fight-or-flight is the best-known response that the hypothalamus can trigger. Less well known is the rest-and-digest response. We can't be on high alert all the time. Sometimes we need to chill. Fight-or-flight is like hitting the accelerator on a car, while rest-and-digest is like tapping the brakes. Your heart rate drops, and your muscles relax. Either way, the hypothalamus sends all those signals.

If you feel overwhelmed or hopeless, fighting or running might not make sense. Instead you might need to calm down. Crying stimulates the rest-and-digest response. One study measured how relaxed people were after watching a sad movie. Mentally healthy people (people without any mood disorders) who cried during the movie were more relaxed afterward

than healthy people who didn't cry. For them, the tears were relaxing.

The researchers also looked at depressed patients. None of the depressed patients, whether they cried or not, were more relaxed after the movie. This could mean that crying doesn't provide much, if any, relief for people with depression. Depression might somehow block crying from triggering rest-and-digest through the hypothalamus.

The rest-and-digest response is one theory about what happens in our brains when we cry. However, it leaves out a huge chunk of what's going on. What's missing? Other people. Crying usually isn't just about one person. It often involves relationships with others. To really understand crying, we have to understand how it works between people.

The word *hippocampus* comes from the ancient Greek word *hippocampus*. *Hippo* means "horse," and *kampos* means "sea monster." In other words, a seahorse. The hippocampus got its name because it's shaped like a seahorse.

"THE EXCREMENTITIOUS HUMIDITIE OF THE BRAYNE"

The Greek physician Hippocrates is credited with developing the theory that the human body contains four important liquids, or "humors." The four humors were blood, yellow bile, black bile, and phlegm. Hippocrates thought illnesses were caused by an imbalance of these humors. Therefore, to maintain health, you just needed to maintain the right balance of humors. Got a fever? Have some leeches drink your blood and you'll feel better in no time! The old word for depression, *melancholy*, actually meant "black bile." The prescribed cure was to remove that extra bile by feeding the patient foods that would have laxative effects. But balancing humors is bad medicine. Don't try it!

It sounds crazy today, but these ideas influenced medicine for about 2,000 years. People believed that crying resulted from too much phlegm in the brain. In 1586 the physician Timothy Bright wrote that crying was good for health because it releases "the excrementitious humiditie of the brayne."

Fortunately, medicine has moved beyond leeches and "excrementitious humiditie." This is a good reminder that science is always changing as we make new discoveries. We know more about the human body than we've ever known before. But we still have far to go, even with something as basic as crying.

CHAPTER 4

The Crying Connection

PICTURE THIS: You're sitting at a lunch table with a group of friends. Everything's fine (you think). Everyone's talking. And then, all of a sudden, one of your friends starts to cry. Everything stops. Whatever you and your friends were talking about is put aside—this has your full attention. That's how crying is—it's impossible to ignore.

Talking Tears

To cry is human. And what do humans do more than any other creature on earth? We socialize. We talk, we text, we pass notes. Even without words, from the moment we're born, we're often communicating. Want to let your brother know that you're mad at him? You could say, "I'm mad at you," or you could just give him some serious stink eye. The stink eye might even work better. Our eyes speak. And of course, that's right where our tears form.

Tears by themselves don't communicate a lot of information. They are like exclamation points. They say, "THIS IS IMPORTANT!!!!!!" Tears often grab another person's attention and create a chance for bonding.

Back to your friend in the lunchroom. Your friend is crying. What do you do? You'll probably try to find out what's wrong. You offer support and ask whether you can help. If you can't help, you listen. You let your friend know that you understand. Maybe you try for a smile. You hope to connect.

Tears often grab another person's attention and create a chance for bonding.

Young kids cry when they are in pain, probably because they can expect to get help. But as we get older, we're more likely to help ourselves when we get hurt. We're less likely to cry from pain. However, older people are more likely to cry about other things. The big causes for adults are loss, conflict, and rejection (especially by someone close to us).

Imagine that a stranger says something rude to you. It might upset you or it might not. But what if your best friend says the mean thing? That would really get to you. It would be more likely to make you cry. That's because your best friend is an important social connection. This is why the people we care about are the most likely to make us cry.

We often cry when we lose an important social connection. We also cry when we feel like we don't have enough social connections. That's when we feel abandoned, hopeless, or overwhelmed. Tears announce that we need help and encourage other people to provide it.

Hold on. There's one problem with this. What about crying alone? If tears are for communication, why would we cry alone? Well, first, tears come from our feelings, and when we're alone, we feel safe to let out those feelings. Also, the fact that you're physically alone doesn't mean that nobody is there in spirit. Maybe you have your pet with you, a favorite stuffed animal, or a letter or picture from

"Crying is above all a relationship behavior, a way to help us get close and not simply a vehicle for emotional expression or release. We do not cry because we need to get rid of pain, but because we need connection. . . . Crying is not about what we let out but about whom we let in."

Judith Kay Nelson,
psychotherapist, teacher, and writer

someone you care about. Chances are good that even if you are technically alone, you're still thinking of someone. Or maybe no one is there, but you wish someone were.

Tears promote empathy between people. Empathy is the ability to understand and share the feelings of others. Tears reveal the internal emotional state of the person who is crying. In the example of your crying friend, the tears caused you to stop what you were doing and empathize, creating a stronger emotional bond. When we empathize with someone who is crying, we might even cry ourselves. Empathetic crying shows the crying person that we truly do feel what he or she is feeling.

Context Changes Everything

So it's all good, right? We cry, someone consoles us, and we feel better. Unfortunately, it's not that simple. When crying works, it can create those bonds. But it can also cause negative reactions.

In 2008 Hillary Clinton was campaigning for the Democratic nomination for president. At one point in an interview, she became emotional. Some reporters said tears welled up in her eyes. Whether or not that was true, those tears made the news. And people had two very different reactions to her crying. Some people saw the tears as proof that Clinton cared deeply about making the country a better place. Others claimed that Clinton was faking it. In addition, some suggested that her tears proved she was weak.

Social context changes how people react to crying. If your best friend is crying, you'll probably stop and try to connect with him or her. If a stranger is crying, you'll still notice, but you might not know what to do. Should you try to help or just leave the person alone? If you see someone you don't get along with crying, you might feel sorry for that person, or you might not. Crying can be a kind of distance regulator—it can bring some people closer while pushing others away.

If you see someone crying and you don't know what to do, start with empathy. Imagine what that person must be feeling. Then ask yourself, "What would I want someone to do?" It might make sense to gently say that you can be there to listen, but that you understand if that person wants to be left alone. Sometimes people want to be left alone, but might feel better just knowing that someone cared enough to offer help. If you think a situation might be dangerous for you or the person crying, ask an adult to help.

Here are some things you might say to someone who is crying:

"It's okay to cry."

"I'm sorry you're hurting. Can I help?"

"Do you need me to get someone to help?"

"Do you need a tissue?"

"If you want to talk to someone, I'm here."

(When) Does It Make You Feel Better?

Popular wisdom says that crying helps. In magazine articles, there is advice such as "Let it out. You'll feel better." But does crying really help? The science is less certain. In most survey studies of crying (in which people are asked whether crying in the past made them feel better), participants usually say crying helped. But in laboratory studies (in which people cry during the study and report their feelings), people usually say crying didn't help. In fact, crying often made them feel worse.

The most common idea about the benefit of crying is that it provides catharsis. This is the idea that we need to release built-up emotions. If we don't, they could build up and explode in unhealthy ways. The idea of catharsis has been around for more than 2,000 years. Aristotle wrote that crying "cleanses the mind." The founder of modern psychology, Sigmund Freud, used the idea of catharsis. He developed the idea that talking with patients could help them relive bad experiences and then move beyond them. There could be some truth to cathartic crying, but scientific studies haven't been able to prove a connection.

The problem might be that we're asking the wrong question. Ad Vingerhoets, a researcher and expert on crying, writes that instead of asking whether crying is good or bad, we should ask "for whom and under what conditions crying is likely to be beneficial." In other words, don't ask whether crying is good. Instead ask, "*When* is crying good?"

Vingerhoets and other researchers have come up with four main variables that can affect the results of crying:

- **Who are the criers?** Are they male or female? What is their health status? What is their personality? Are they outgoing or shy?

- **What caused the crying?** Is it something the crier can control, or is it impossible to fix?

- **What kind of crying is it?** A single tear? Uncontrollable sobbing?

- **How do others react?** What do other people think of the crying? Did anyone respond with empathy?

Let's look at just one variable—how others react. If a boy cries a few tears at home because his older brother said something mean, and the brother responds with a sincere apology, then crying will probably help the boy feel better. If the boy sobs loudly in front of kids who make fun of him for it, then crying probably won't help. In this case, crying isn't helpful when others ignore or laugh at the boy. But crying is helpful when it connects the boy to someone who reacts with empathy and tries to help.

Boys Don't Cry?

Let's look a little more closely at another of those variables. Is the crying person male or female? Your gender can affect whether or not you feel better after crying. It may sound weird, but if you think about it, it makes sense.

Does society treat male and female tears the same? Not always. In some ways, society considers crying a "female" activity. Girls are believed to cry more often. But do they really? Studies show that, starting around 8 to 11 years of age, girls cry more often than boys.

There are two basic explanations: nature and nurture. If you do something because of nature, it's just what comes naturally. If you do something because of nurture, it's your learned behavior.

Researchers have some theories about how the difference in crying might be a matter of nature. If girls are naturally more in touch with their own emotions and the emotions of others, then girls might cry more often than boys.

Our hormones also play a natural role in our emotions. Some scientists think the female sex hormones prolactin and estrogen make girls and women more likely to cry than boys and men. Research also suggests that the male sex hormone testosterone makes males less likely to cry. These hormones don't directly cause crying. Instead, they change the likelihood that we will cry. Imagine a glass that holds our emotions. If it gets too full, we cry. Prolactin might make the glass smaller, while testosterone might make it bigger. (Other things can also change our crying threshold, such as whether we are sick or haven't gotten enough sleep).

If the difference in crying is caused by nurture, however, then males and females cry at different rates because that's what society expects. If boys keep hearing that boys don't cry, they probably learn to hold it in.

Both reasons could be partly true. One study looked at rates of crying in 37 countries around the world. In every culture studied, women reported crying more often. However, in some countries the difference was very small—almost nonexistent. Also, if the men thought they shouldn't cry, then they might report less crying. In that case, the difference is in the reporting, not the true numbers.

There's another explanation for why women might cry more than men. Some experts think we have a stress reaction called "tend and befriend." For women more often than men, fight-or-flight isn't always an option. If a woman with young children is in a dangerous situation, her first instinct might be to protect the kids. Fight-or-flight might not work, but it's no time to rest-and-digest. Instead she needs to find help. "Tend and befriend" means taking care of your connections and making new ones. Men can tend and befriend too, but it might come more naturally to women. Or maybe women tend and befriend more because society—nurture—expects it. The truth is probably a mix of both.

Either way, if anyone ever tells you that boys don't cry, don't believe it. Boys and girls can be different in how, when, and why they cry. But that's just how people are. People's crying behavior varies, but we all cry, and that is nature.

"Crying's always been a way for me to get things out which are buried deep, deep down. When I sing, I often cry. Crying is feeling, and feeling is being human. Oh yes, I cry."

Ray Charles,
The Genius of Soul

Don't Judge (Yourself)!

Society can also affect how we think about our crying. How we think about it makes a difference in how crying feels. If we are embarrassed by our tears, they might make us feel worse. But if we believe we have a right to our feelings, then those tears are more likely to make us feel better.

We can't control other people, but we can decide how we treat ourselves. We feel empathy when our friends cry, so we should also give ourselves a break when our own tears show up. When we do, those tears are more likely to help.

Sometimes it makes sense to hold in our tears. Other times, when it feels safe, it feels good to let it out. One of the most important factors is social. A study found that the presence of a single close person while crying was most likely to improve someone's mood. The presence of a group of people was more likely to make the crier feel worse. We don't want to share our personal feelings with the whole world. This is one reason we sometimes cry alone; we don't always have a close friend or family member nearby to connect with. But we want to share our feelings with somebody, preferably somebody we are close to. Sometimes we all need a good shoulder to cry on.

HOLDING IT IN

We've established that crying can be helpful, but sometimes you might want to save the tears for later, especially if you are in a big peer group. If so, here are a few tips:

- **Relax your face.** You use your facial muscles to cry. Before you start crying, these muscles tense up. Loosening them pushes the tears back.
- **Press your tongue against the roof of your mouth.** Imagine that you have a secret "Stop Crying" button in your mouth that you can push with your tongue. Sipping water, swallowing, or yawning can have the same effect.
- **Breathe.** Pay attention to your breathing and slow it down. Try slowly counting to four as you breathe in, then counting to four again as you breathe out. Repeat as needed.
- **Walk away.** If you can take yourself out of the situation, you can control your emotions. If you can't walk away physically, you can leave mentally. Replace your sad thoughts with something positive.

These tips for postponing crying may work. But if you start to cry, something important might be going on. You can save it for later, but don't ignore it! Bottling up emotions isn't a good way to deal with them.

ARE THERE FAKE TEARS?

Tears are often seen as proof of someone's honesty. It's often said that "the eyes are windows to the soul." If a person cries while telling a sad story, he or she is more likely to be believed. But can people fake tears? For sure.

One profession—acting—pays people who can cry on demand. Many actors claim to be able to cry on cue. Emma Watson, who played Hermione Granger in the Harry Potter films, has been quoted as saying that in order to cry, "I think about sad memories and if I don't manage to cry, then I cry out of frustration." She has a main method for crying *and* a backup. Either way, she knows how to bring on the tears on cue. To get into the mood for crying, many actors recall sad memories. Some even say they're so in touch with their emotions that just remembering what feeling sad is like makes the tears flow.

If the sadness is real, then are the tears really fake? Maybe not. However, even if the tears themselves aren't fake, they *can* be used to trick someone (as in a movie).

CRYING WITH A "HANDSOME" MAN

How we view crying is partly a result of our culture. Some cultures are OK with crying. Others think people shouldn't cry. Japan is known as a very reserved country, where emotions are often hidden.

A recent National Geographic short film explored Japanese culture and crying. In Japan, someone started a business where women can pay to cry with a "handsome" man. They watch a video designed to get the tears flowing. As they shed tears, a good-looking man gently dabs their cheeks with a handkerchief. If the women can't cry, the man cries for them, to help them get started.

These women want to cry with someone. In a country like Japan, where it can be risky to show your feelings, there are few places where people can have a good cry. If all they want is to cry alone, they could rent a sad movie. But having a handsome man there gives the women a chance to make a connection while crying. As the owner of the company says in the film, "This is a chance to show their crying face to each other."

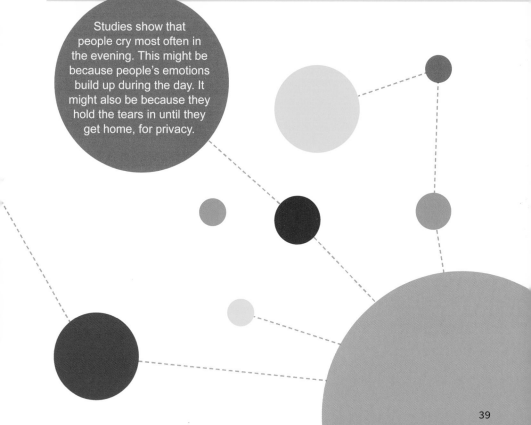

Studies show that people cry most often in the evening. This might be because people's emotions build up during the day. It might also be because they hold the tears in until they get home, for privacy.

CHAPTER 5

When the Tears Aren't Working

CRYING IS AN IMPORTANT PART of who we are. It helps us to maintain human connections, especially at critical moments. The connections can bring great relief and help us feel better. But sometimes nothing—not even crying—seems to help.

Depression

Imagine that you live under water. You can still breathe, but everything else is a lot harder. Just walking around can feel almost impossible. Everything seems murky or far away. Sometimes this is what depression is like.

Depression doesn't necessarily mean too many tears. People with mild forms of depression may cry uncontrollably, but people with more severe depression might not cry at all, even when they want to. Either way, depressed people feel disconnected from the world.

SOME COMMON SIGNS OF DEPRESSION

- Feeling sad or empty most of the time (sadness may show itself as extreme irritability)
- Loss of interest in activities that used to be fun
- Weight loss or weight gain (usually a gain or loss of 5 percent of body weight)
- Getting too little or too much sleep
- Low energy most of the time
- Feeling worthless or guilty for no reason
- Trouble concentrating or making decisions
- Frequent thoughts of death or self-harm

Someone who has five or more of these symptoms for two or more weeks might be suffering with depression. A major difference between depression and sadness is that, when you're depressed, these negative feelings don't go away quickly.

Psst! Hey Neuron, Pass This Note to Amy(gdala)

Depression and other mood disorders are medical conditions. They are often signs that the limbic system is not working correctly. To see how that works, you need to understand how the brain sends messages. How does the limbic system get its messages to the lacrimal system? The messages travel through the neurons (nerve cells).

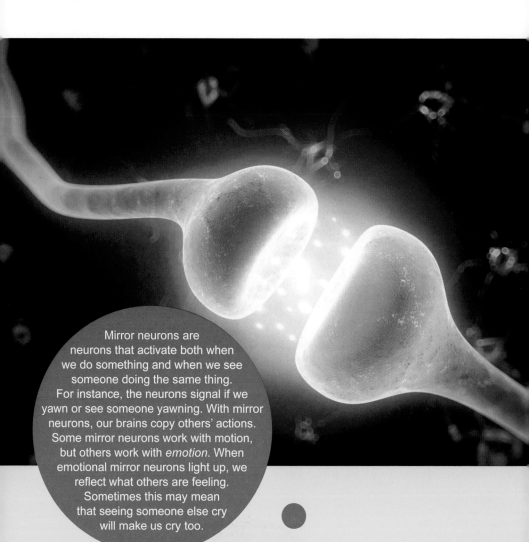

Mirror neurons are neurons that activate both when we do something and when we see someone doing the same thing. For instance, the neurons signal if we yawn or see someone yawning. With mirror neurons, our brains copy others' actions. Some mirror neurons work with motion, but others work with *emotion*. When emotional mirror neurons light up, we reflect what others are feeling. Sometimes this may mean that seeing someone else cry will make us cry too.

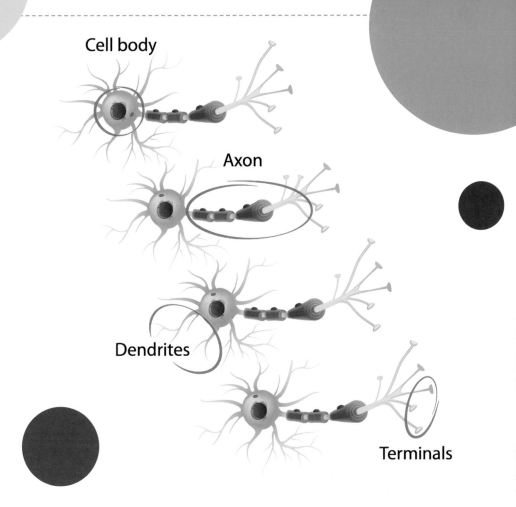

Cell body

Axon

Dendrites

Terminals

Here's how that goes:

- Neurons have short, branched extensions called dendrites. They send signals to the cell body.
- From the cell body, the signals go down the long axon.
- The axon ends with a network of small branches.
- Each small branch ends in a terminal that forms a synapse (junction) with the next neuron's dendrite.

Neurotransmitters, which are chemicals used by the brain, carry messages from one neuron to the next. When the next cell receives the neurotransmitters, it forwards them along.

If your limbic system has trouble communicating, your moods can suffer. Research suggests that depression might be caused when parts of the brain are struggling to communicate correctly. This possibility makes sense—how can the system work if it can't communicate?

Have you ever had a miscommunication with a friend? Maybe the friend was upset about something, but you thought he or she was mad at *you*. And then maybe you got mad at your friend. Once you talked it out, you both realized there was nothing to be mad about. To get along, we need to communicate. Our brains can seem to work in a similar way. When parts of the brain struggle to communicate, we struggle too. To see how that works, let's consider what can happen in the brain of a depressed person.

In a study, researchers used magnetic resonance imaging (MRI) to measure the size of people's hippocampi. In the people who had a history of depression, the hippocampus was 9 to 13 percent smaller. Part of their amygdala was also smaller. Those size differences could be the result of damaged neurons. Neurons in depressed patients might have fewer connections than neurons in people without depression.

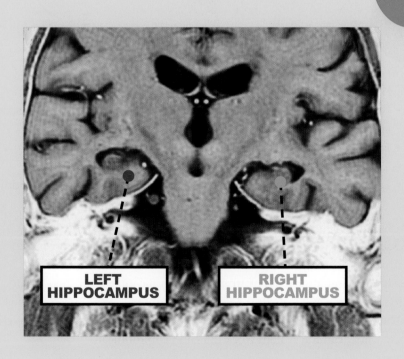

LEFT
HIPPOCAMPUS

RIGHT
HIPPOCAMPUS

Research suggests that hormones released when we experience stress can impair the growth of neurons. Too much stress damages the neurons, making it harder for the limbic system to send messages. If this is true, then emotional stress could cause physical changes in the brain that lead to depression.

It's a vicious cycle. Stress may lead to changes in the brain, which can lead to depression, which then leads to more stress . . . and on and on. That's not fair! No one should have to get stuck like that. Fortunately, understanding the cause of the problem helps doctors figure out ways to make it better.

Researchers are constantly looking for new ways to help patients break out of these cycles.

Many of the antidepressant medications used to treat depression increase the amount of neurotransmitters floating between the neurons. This should make it easier for the parts of the limbic system to communicate. One theory says the extra neurotransmitters help neurons grow. So stress hormones might impair the growth of neurons, but adding certain neurotransmitters might help to repair the damage.

A study found that depressed people had below-average activity in their amygdalas when they thought of positive memories. But they had above-average activity when they thought of negative memories. So their brains struggled to think of positive things and got stuck on the negative. Imagine a car deep in mud with its tires spinning. The wheels turn and turn and just get deeper and deeper in the muck. That's what these patients' brains were doing.

Researchers are constantly looking for new ways to help patients break out of these cycles. Let's look at two of those ways, one very new and one very old.

Thinking About Thinking: Neurofeedback and Mindfulness

Some patients with depression were shown live MRI images of their amygdalas in a study. As they were remembering positive events, they could actually watch their brains think happy thoughts. They were then taught how to consciously train their amygdalas to be more positive. Their symptoms of depression went down. This type of training, where you can see and respond to what your brain is doing, is called neurofeedback.

Even without MRI scans, you can still see what's going on in your head. After all, it's *your* head—you're already

in there. You just have to pay attention. Paying attention to your thoughts and feelings is sometimes called mindfulness. When we get caught up in our stressful lives, we're not paying attention. Sometimes we just get stuck. We think about homework, the next test, who we'll sit with at lunch, how our parents are *so annoying*. It can go on and on. It's a little like a hamster running on a wheel, round and round, going nowhere. Sometimes we are the hamster (especially when we're stressed). Mindfulness is about stepping off the hamster wheel and letting our minds reset.

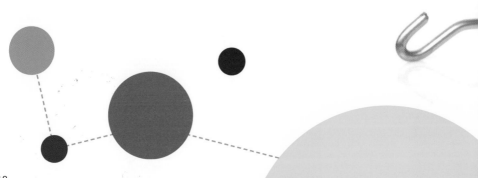

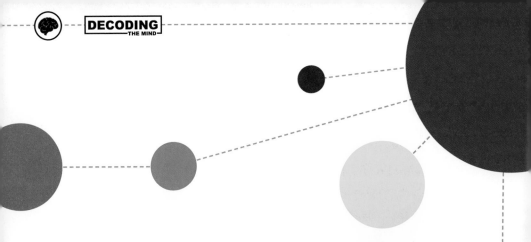

The practice of mindfulness is thousands of years old. Try it for a second. Think about what you've been thinking about lately. Were you stuck on a negative cycle? No judging now! If we get mad at ourselves for having negative thoughts, we're still on that wheel. Mindfulness is about being aware of our feelings, not judging them. This practice may help you relax enough to release your tension and let out tears you were holding back. This is a good thing!

All by itself, mindfulness can help to lessen stress. With practice, you can learn how to catch yourself when negative thoughts begin to take over. You can spend less and less time on that wheel to nowhere.

The science is complicated, but some studies have found that mindfulness training leads to more gray matter (nerve tissue) in the hippocampus and reduces stress hormones. We can't all hook our heads up to an MRI, but if we want to be happier, we *can* train our brains.

. . . if we want to be happier, we *can* train our brains.

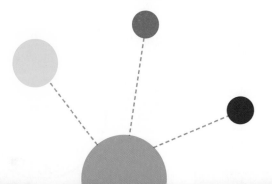

It's More Common Than You Think

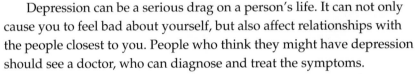

Depression can be a serious drag on a person's life. It can not only cause you to feel bad about yourself, but also affect relationships with the people closest to you. People who think they might have depression should see a doctor, who can diagnose and treat the symptoms.

One study conducted between 2009 and 2012 found that almost 6 percent of kids ages 12 to 17 had depression. That's more than one in 20 teens. According to another study, between 2005 and 2014 the depression rate among adolescents rose 37 percent. (Researchers think the increase was driven by the use of digital tools, such as smartphones and social media.) Clearly a lot of teens are feeling depressed. But there's hope! Proper treatment can help.

A trained medical professional is needed to make sure a severely depressed patient gets the best treatment. There are two basic kinds of treatments for depression—behavior therapy and medication.

Behavior therapy involves talking with a trained counselor. Having someone to talk to can be a huge help. After all, humans may have evolved to cry emotional tears to make sure we had someone to talk to when we needed it most. Just as we all cry sometimes, we all occasionally need help. That's not a bad sign! It just means we're human.

People trained in treating depression have many tools to help patients get through it. They know techniques to help their patients avoid negative thought cycles. They know the mental traps that we fall into and how to avoid them. Most of all, they know how to listen and provide support.

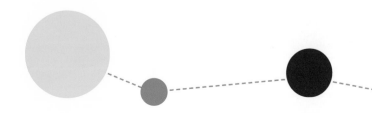

No one should have to suffer alone.

After behavior therapy, medication is another option. Antidepressants work by changing the amount of neurotransmitters between the neurons. It's possible that they fix stress-caused damage by helping the neurons grow and communicate.

No one should have to suffer alone. If you think you or someone you know has depression, you should reach out. Help is out there.

Shrinking Sadness

Sadness is a part of life, like skinned knees and getting the flu. However, there are some basic things that we can all do to feel happier most of the time.

- **EAT HEALTHILY:** Eating a giant bag of chips and some ice cream might feel good at first, but an hour later? Not so much. Eating a healthy diet with lots of fruits and veggies helps keep our bodies, including our brains, in top shape. When we're healthy, we're more likely to feel happy.

- **EXERCISE:** Exercise gives us more energy, healthier bodies and minds, stronger self-esteem, and better sleep. What's not to like? Of course, everything in moderation—don't overdo it!

- **GET OUTSIDE:** This could go along with getting exercise. Getting out into nature gives us a chance to stop negative thinking and calm our emotions.

- **BE MINDFUL:** Being aware of our thoughts can lead to happier minds. When we think about what we're thinking, without judging those thoughts, we get a chance to stop thinking in negative circles.

- **GET GOOD SLEEP:** Nothing can reset our mood like a good night's sleep. There's no one trick to getting good sleep, but there are lots of little things we can do to increase the chances. They include following the same bedtime routine every night, avoiding caffeinated drinks and chocolate near bedtime, and turning off ALL electronics well before bedtime. But just as insufficient sleep can disrupt your mood, too much sleep can do it too. Kids from 6 to 12 years old usually need 9 to 12 hours of sleep.

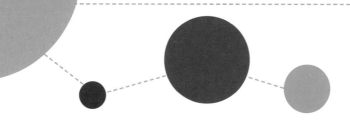

- **TURN IT OFF:** Our electronic gadgets can be fun, but they can also hijack our brains. Video games, phones, tablets, computers, TV—they all can be too stimulating. So be sure to disconnect from the digital world sometimes and connect with real life.

- **GET CREATIVE:** Art is a great way to express your feelings. You could try writing a poem or drawing a picture about how you feel. Keeping a journal can also help.

- **SPEND TIME WITH A PET:** Being with a pet can lower stress.

- **BE THANKFUL:** If you make a habit of being thankful, it can help you feel more positive. You might start your day with a gratitude list or end your day with a list of things that went well. Practicing gratefulness is a healthy habit. Of course, on some days you might not be feeling grateful. If it sometimes feels like too much, don't sweat it.

Nothing will make you happy all the time. In fact, it wouldn't even make sense to feel only happiness and no other emotions. Life comes with ups and downs. So while these tips won't make you feel happy all the time, they can help you cope when life gets you down.

For something more serious, like depression, these might be more like Band-Aids than full-on treatment. So if you think you might have more than normal sadness, seek help from a medical professional. You can start with a school nurse or counselor to help you find the right resources.

"I cry often and easily. I think you're supposed to feel all kinds of things. You're supposed to laugh, you're supposed to cry, you're not supposed to shove your feelings under the rug."

Ellen DeGeneres, comedian, actor, and TV host

CHAPTER 6

Conclusion:
All Mixed Up

A LL RIGHT, ENOUGH SADNESS! What about happiness? Can you think of the happiest thing that ever happened to you? Maybe you were struggling in a class but you managed to get a good grade on the final test. Or maybe it was the first sight of your mom after she returned from a business trip. Whatever it was, it was probably something that came after a struggle. You worked really hard, you had some bad days, but you got through it, and it felt great. The happiest times in our lives wouldn't be possible without some of the hardest.

That might be why people cry sometimes at their happiest moments. Maybe they're remembering the struggle. Maybe they're thinking of all the sad things they went through to get to that moment. Without the sadness, the joy wouldn't be so strong.

In fact, sometimes our strongest emotions—the ones that really let us know that we're alive and important and that life matters—don't fit into neat little boxes. Laughter can carry great sadness, tears great joy. When people share these strong, mixed-up emotions, we make meaningful bonds (often with tears in our eyes). Maybe this is why we seek out sad movies and books; they are a safe, easy way to remind us of our connections to others and to experience our own humanity.

So if you're reading a Harry Potter book and a certain character dies while saving Harry, or if you're watching *Moana* and she and her grandmother share a special moment, don't feel bad if you cry. It's only natural. And when something happens in real life to make you cry, know that those tears matter. Whether it makes more sense to let them out right away or wait until later, your mind and your body are saying, "This is important!" Be sure to listen. Think about what those tears mean. What made you cry? What were you feeling when the tears came on? Acknowledging and understanding your own emotions makes you braver and stronger.

And if you see someone else crying, try to imagine what he or she is feeling. When we empathize with each other, we're doing our best at being human.

Reach Out

The hardest part of any journey might be the first steps. The hardest part of getting through depression might be asking for help (or, if you're worried about a friend who might be depressed, asking whether he or she needs help). Taking those first steps, seeking help, is so important. Help is out there.

If you think you or someone you know might be suffering from depression:

SEEK HELP. The first step toward treatment might be finding someone to talk to. That person could be a friend, teacher, or family member. It could be someone in your religious community. It could be a neighbor or a coach. Whoever it is, it's important to reach out. People who care are out there. Treatments are out there. Taking this first step will help you find them.

If you think you or someone you know might deliberately do something dangerous, or even life-threatening:

DON'T WAIT. It's important to get help right away. The National Suicide Prevention Lifeline is a free, confidential service that you can call to talk to a counselor right away.

The phone number is 1-800-273-TALK (1-800-273-8255).

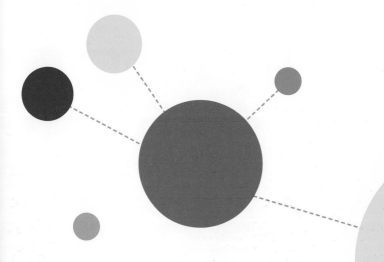

Glossary

anecdotal—based on a personal account that has not been scientifically studied

antidepressants—drugs used to treat depression and other mood disorders; most antidepressants work by changing the amount of neurotransmitters between the neurons

catharsis—the process of releasing strong emotions that is supposed to bring relief

depression—long-term feelings of extreme sadness; a medical condition that should be treated by a mental health professional

empathy—the ability to understand and share another's feelings

endocrine system—the body system that controls our hormones

homeostasis—a state of being balanced physically and emotionally

hormone—a chemical that travels in the blood and regulates such things as cell growth and changes in behavior or mood

intentional—done in hopes of reaching a goal or getting a particular reaction

lacrimal—related to weeping or tears

limbic system—the system of nerves and networks in the brain that controls our emotions

mindfulness—awareness of one's mental state

MRI—magnetic resonance imaging; an MRI scanner uses strong magnetic and radio waves to create detailed images of the inside of the body, including the inside of the brain; an MRI scan can detect activity in particular areas of the brain

neurofeedback—a process in which a person's brain activity can be displayed, allowing the person to learn to control the activity

neuron—a nerve cell that transmits information

neurotransmitter—a chemical substance released by neurons to help them communicate

separation anxiety—feeling scared or nervous when kept apart from a parent, caregiver, or familiar surroundings

symptom—a physical or mental effect of a disease

Additional Resources

Further Reading

Crist, James J. *What to Do When You're Cranky & Blue: A Guide for Kids.* Minneapolis: Free Spirit, 2014.

Eben Field, Jon. *Depression and Other Mood Disorders.* New York: Crabtree, 2014.

Legrand, Claire. *Some Kind of Happiness.* New York: Simon & Schuster Books for Young Readers, 2017.

Poole, Hilary W. *Depression.* Broomall, PA: Mason Crest, 2015.

Internet Sites

Dealing with Depression
http://dwdonline.ca/

Mindfulness for Teens
http://mindfulnessforteens.com/

Teenager's Guide to Depression
https://helpguide.org/articles/depression/
teenagers-guide-to-depression.htm

Critical Thinking Questions

1

According to Darwin's theory of evolution, traits that help a species survive are naturally selected. Those traits tend to spread through a population. For example, if being tall helps giraffes survive, then over many generations, giraffes grow taller. Humans may be the only species that has evolved to produce emotional tears. What are some reasons that emotional tears might help humans survive? What other human traits make tears beneficial? Do you think being able to cry would be beneficial to other animals? What kind of animals, and why?

2

Imagine something that might make a person cry. It can be real or made up. Does it have to do with a person's social connections in any way? If so, how? Now imagine that a friend of yours was crying for that reason. What might you do to help your friend feel better?

3

Imagine that the parts of the limbic system discussed in this book (the hippocampus, hypothalamus, amygdala, and thalamus) are characters with their own personalities. Based on their roles in the brain, what would they be like? How would they handle a stressful situation? Try writing a conversation that they might have about such a situation.

Source Notes

p. 13, "The first step to connection . . ." Sabrina Benaim. *Depression & Other Magic Tricks.* Minneapolis: Button Poetry, 2017, introduction.

p. 15, "more than just a logo . . ." NBA, "Michael Jordan Receives the Presidential Medal of Freedom," YouTube, November 22, 2016, https://www.youtube.com/watch?v=UTWvhpd6Qpo Accessed April 4, 2019.

p. 23, "The excrementitious humiditie . . ." Tom Lutz. *Crying: The Natural and Cultural History of Tears.* New York: W. W. Norton, 1999, p. 73.

p. 26, "Crying is above all a relationship behavior . . ." Judith Kay Nelson. *Seeing Through Tears: Crying and Attachment.* Abingdon, UK: Taylor and Francis, 2012, p. 6.

p. 31, "For whom and under what conditions . . ." A. J. J. M. Vingerhoets. *Why Only Humans Weep: Unravelling the Mysteries of Tears.* Oxford: Oxford University Press, 2013, p. 106.

p. 35, "Crying's always been a way for me . . ." Ray Charles and David Ritz. *Brother Ray: Ray Charles' Own Story.* Boston: Da Capo, 1978, p. 25.

p. 38, "I think about sad memories . . ." John Hopewell, "San Sebastian: Alejandro Amenabar on Ethan Hawke, Emma Watson, 'Regression.'" *Variety,* September 18, 2015, https://variety.com/2015/film/festivals/san-sebastian-alejandro-amenabar-on-ethan-hawke-emma-watson-regression-1201596953/ Accessed April 4, 2019.

p. 39, "This is a chance to show . . ." Darryl Thoms, "See Why Japanese Women Are Paying to Cry with a 'Handsome' Man," National Geographic Society, Short Film Showcase, January 15, 2018, https://news.nationalgeographic.com/2018/01/japan-crying-culture-women-handsome/ Accessed April 4, 2019.

p. 55, "I cry often and easily . . ." Ellen DeGeneres, "Oprah Talks to Ellen DeGeneres," http://www.oprah.com/omagazine/Oprah-Interviews-Ellen-DeGeneres-Ellens-O-Magazine-Cover/3 Accessed April 4, 2019.

Select Bibliography

Bahadur, Nina, "How to Stop Yourself From Crying," *The New York Times*, October 14, 2018, www.nytimes.com/2018/10/14/well/mind/how-to-stop-yourself-from-crying.html Accessed April 4, 2019.

Sabrina Benaim. *Depression & Other Magic Tricks*. Minneapolis: Button Poetry, 2017.

Diagnostic and Statistical Manual of Mental Disorders: DSM-5. Washington, DC: American Psychiatric Publishing, 2013.

Charles, Ray, and David Ritz. *Brother Ray: Ray Charles' Own Story*. Boston: Da Capo, 1978.

Ellen DeGeneres, "Oprah Talks to Ellen DeGeneres," http://www.oprah.com/omagazine/Oprah-Interviews-Ellen-DeGeneres-Ellens-O-Magazine-Cover/3 Accessed April 4, 2019.

Hess, Amanda, "Crying Jordan: The Meme That Just Won't Die," *The New York Times*, December 21, 2017, www.nytimes.com/2016/06/04/arts/crying-jordan-the-meme-that-just-wont-die.html Accessed April 4, 2019.

Hopewell, John, "San Sebastian: Alejandro Amenabar on Ethan Hawke, Emma Watson, 'Regression,'" *Variety*, September 18, 2015, https://variety.com/2015/film/festivals/san-sebastian-alejandro-amenabar-on-ethan-hawke-emma-watson-regression-1201596953/ Accessed April 4, 2019.

King, Barbara J. *How Animals Grieve*. Chicago: University of Chicago Press, 2014.

Lutz, Tom. *Crying: The Natural and Cultural History of Tears*. New York: W. W. Norton, 1999.

NBA, "Michael Jordan Receives the Presidential Medal of Freedom," YouTube, November 22, 2016, www.youtube.com/watch?v=UTWvhpd6Qpo Accessed April 4, 2019.

Nelson, Judith Kay. *Seeing Through Tears: Crying and Attachment*. Abingdon, UK: Taylor and Francis, 2012.

Pratt, Laura A., and Debra J. Brody, "Depression in the U.S. Household Population, 2009–2012," Centers for Disease Control and Prevention, December 3, 2014, www.cdc.gov/nchs/data/databriefs/db172.htm Accessed April 4, 2019.

Sugarman, Joe, "The Rise of Teen Depression," *Johns Hopkins Health Review* 4, No. 2 (Fall–Winter 2017), www.johnshopkinshealthreview.com/issues/fall-winter-2017/articles/the-rise-of-teen-depression Accessed April 4, 2019.

Thoms, Darryl, "See Why Japanese Women Are Paying to Cry with a 'Handsome' Man," National Geographic Society, Short Film Showcase, January 15, 2018, https://news.nationalgeographic.com/2018/01/japan-crying-culture-women-handsome/ Accessed April 4, 2019.

Trimble, Michael R. *Why Humans Like to Cry: Tragedy, Evolution, and the Brain*. Oxford: Oxford University Press, 2014.

Vingerhoets, A. J. J. M. *Why Only Humans Weep: Unravelling the Mysteries of Tears*. Oxford: Oxford University Press, 2013.

Index

About the Author

Matt Lilley lives and writes in Minneapolis, Minnesota. He has written five books for young people. His favorite topics to write about include health issues, nature, and exploration. He loves learning about topics in science and sharing that knowledge. Matt has a master's degree in scientific and technical communication. He is also a Minnesota Master Naturalist. He loves going out in nature and seeing what's out there. To find out more about Matt, visit him at mattlilley.ink.